Phonological Awareness
Quick Checks

Table of Contents

Introduction

The Goal of Quick Checks: Program Overview

The *Benchmark Advance* program has ten units per grade in Grades K–2. There are ten knowledge strands on which the program revolves. Each three-week unit focuses on a Unit Topic and an Essential Question, which both relate back to the overall knowledge strand. Throughout the school year, students engage with texts in whole- and small-group settings, developing their phonics skills and applying the new strategies in context.

The *Phonological Awareness* assessments are designed to help you evaluate your students' awareness of key phonological concepts. They also provide a regularly administered and consistent tool for determining when it may be appropriate to use intervention materials with struggling students. Below are the key resources within *Benchmark Advance* used in the intervention cycle and a description of how these components relate to one another.

The Teacher's Resource System and associated student reading serve as the core of the *Benchmark Advance* program. This material supports day-to-day instruction throughout the school year.

Foundational Skills Screeners consists of quick tests focused on foundational reading skills, including recognizing root words, identifying affixes, and recognizing sound patterns. *Foundational Skills Screeners* provides an efficient way to assess the general understanding of the class. Based on students' scores, you can shape instruction to meet developing areas of need before students fall behind.

The four Grades K–2 Quick Checks consist of short, skill-based assessments designed to help you evaluate students' command in key skill and knowledge areas. You may use students' performances on the Quick Checks to inform your decision of when to implement intervention. Look for the Resource Map in each book, which leads you to the exact intervention lesson that reviews the skills assessed in each Quick Check test.

The grade-specific, skill-based lessons in each Intervention book provide you with instruction and practice needed to raise struggling students to on-level proficiency. Designed to integrate with Quick Checks, these intervention resources can be used to pinpoint trouble areas and support students as they build the skill set they need for complete understanding.

Administering the Quick Check Assessments

Phonological awareness is the ability to hear and orally manipulate sounds in spoken language. It includes the recognition of sounds, the ability to hear rhyme, the ability to hear syllables within words, and the ability to hear and manipulate phonemes, or individual sounds, in words. Phonemic awareness is the understanding that the sounds of spoken language work together to make words.

The assessments in this book evaluate students on 15 different skills, including awareness of words and syllables, identifying rhyme, recognizing sounds, differentiating sounds, onset and rime, phoneme segmentation, initial sound substitution, blending phonemes, and forming words. There are two assessment pages for each of the 15 skills. Skills may be assessed at any time and in any sequence, based on what is happening in classroom instruction; there is no need to follow the sequence of the skills as they are ordered in this book.

The *Phonological Awareness* assessments are generally designed to be administered one-on-one, although some of the assessments may be administered in small groups. Each assessment focuses on a single skill. We recommend that you make a copy of the page for each student you plan to assess. Write the student's name at the top of the page. You may administer, score, and record the results of an assessment on the page.

Every assessment is designed to be used twice, if needed. If a student does not do well the first time, you may want to assess the student again. You may administer the same assessment as a pretest and posttest—at the beginning and end of the quarter, for example—or as an initial test and follow-up retest to see how much progress the student has made.

Quick Check to Reading Intervention

Individual responses provide the best information on a particular student's development, and considering responses from the class as a whole helps determine when to move on to new and more difficult tasks. Carefully observe students' behaviors in phonological awareness and other literacy activities, documenting both lessons taught and skills achieved.

Each assessment includes a reproducible score sheet that indicates the number of points possible in each assessment. Assessments include 5 to 10 questions; each question is worth a single point.

Using the Scores to Offer Intervention

Based on your student's score, you may decide to offer the student additional resources as in the *Benchmark Advance* Intervention. The Quick Check to Intervention Resource Map that follows this introduction aligns the skills being assessed to the Reading Intervention lessons.

If the student scores...	Then...
80%–100%	Move on to the next Quick Check or skill.
66%–80%	Consider administering the Quick Check again. Continue monitoring the student during future Quick Checks.
below 66%	Use additional resources shown in the Resource Map to provide the student with opportunities to remediate skills.

Quick Check to Intervention
Resource Map

Skill	Quick Check Number	Benchmark Advance: Phonological Awareness Intervention Lesson	Intervention Lesson Page Number
Recognize Rhyme	1 (p. 2) 2 (p. 3)	**Grade K** Lesson 1: Determine Which Part of a Word Is Important to Rhyming	2
		Lesson 2: Identifying Rhyming Words	4
		Grade 1 Lesson 8: Determine Which Part of a Word Is Important to Rhyming	16
		Lesson 9: Identifying Rhyming Words	18
		Grade 2 Lesson 8: Determine Which Part of a Word Is Important to Rhyming	16
		Lesson 9: Identifying Rhyming Words	18
Produce Rhyme	3 (p. 4) 4 (p. 5)	**Grade K** Lesson 3: Producing Rhyming Words	6
		Grade 1 Lesson 10: Produce Rhyming Words	20
		Grade 2 Lesson 10: Produce Rhyming Words	20
Recognize or Produce Rhyme	5 (p. 6) 6 (p. 7)	**Grade K:** Lesson 1: Determine Which Part of a Word Is Important to Rhyming	2
		Lesson 2: Identify Rhyming Words	4
		Grade 1 Lesson 8: Determine Which Part of a Word Is Important to Rhyming	16
		Lesson 9: Identify Rhyming Words	18
Phoneme Isolation	7 (p. 8) 8 (p. 9)	**Grade K** Lesson 10: Isolate and Pronounce the Initial, Medial, and Final Sounds in Three-Phoneme Words	20
		Grade 1 Lesson 16: Isolate and Pronounce the Initial, Medial, and Final Sounds in Three-Phoneme Words	32
		Grade 2 Lesson 16: Isolate and Pronounce the Initial, Medial, and Final Sounds in Three-Phoneme Words	32
Blend Onset and Rime	9 (p. 10) 10 (p. 11)	**Grade K** Lesson 8: Blend and Segment Onset and Rime	16
		Grade 1 Lesson 15: Blend and Segment Onset and Rime	30
		Grade 2 Lesson 15: Blend and Segment Onset and Rime	30
Syllable Blending	11 (p. 12) 12 (p. 13)	**Grade K** Lesson 4: Blend Spoken Words Together to Make Compound Words	8
		Grade 1 Lesson 11: Blend Spoken Words Together to Make Compound Words	22
		Grade 2 Lesson 11: Blend Spoken Words Together to Make Compound Words	22
Phoneme Segmentation	13 (p. 14) 14 (p. 15)	**Grade K** Lesson 10: Isolate and Pronounce the Initial, Medial, and Final Sounds in Three-Phoneme Words	20
		Grade 1 Lesson 16: Isolate and Pronounce the Initial, Medial, and Final Sounds in Three-Phoneme Words	32
		Grade 2 Lesson 16: Isolate and Pronounce the Initial, Medial, and Final Sounds in Three-Phoneme Words	32

Quick Check to Intervention
Resource Map (continued)

Skill	Quick Check Number	Benchmark Advance: Phonological Awareness Intervention Lesson	Intervention Lesson Page Number
Phoneme Categorization	15 (p. 16)	**Grade 1** Lesson 17: Identify Individual Sounds in Spoken Words	34
	16 (p. 17)	**Grade 2** Lesson 17: Identify Individual Sounds in Spoken Words	34
Initial Sound Substitution	17 (p. 18)	**Grade K** Lesson 13: Produce a Spoken Word When Sounds Are Added or Substituted	26
	18 (p. 19)	**Grade 1** Lesson 19: Produce a Spoken Word When Sounds Are Added or Substituted	38
		Grade 2 Lesson 19: Produce a Spoken Word When Sounds Are Added or Substituted	38
Distinguish Initial Sounds in Spoken Words	19 (p. 20)	**Grade K** Lesson 6: Distinguish Initial Sound in Spoken Words	12
	20 (p. 21)	**Grade 1** Lesson 13: Distinguish Initial Sound in Spoken Words	26
		Grade 2 Lesson 13: Detect Initial Sound in Spoken Words	26
Distinguish Syllables in Spoken Words	21 (p. 22)	**Grade K** Lesson 11: Identify Individual Sounds in Spoken Words	22
	22 (p. 23)	**Grade 1** Lesson 17: Identify Individual Sounds in Spoken Words	34
		Grade 2 Lesson 17: Identify Individual Sounds in Spoken Words	34
Phoneme Blending	23 (p. 24)	**Grade K** Lesson 14: Blend Two to Three Phonemes into Recognizable Words	28
	24 (p. 25)	**Grade 1** Lesson 20: Blend Two to Three Phonemes into Recognizable Words	40
		Grade 2 Lesson 20: Blend Two to Three Phonemes into Recognizable Words	40
Final Sound Substitution	25 (p. 26)	**Grade K** Lesson 13: Produce a Spoken Word When Sounds Are Added or Substituted	26
	26 (p. 27)	**Grade 1** Lesson 19: Produce a Spoken Word When Sounds Are Added or Substituted	38
		Grade 2 Lesson 19: Produce a Spoken Word When Sounds Are Added or Substituted	38
Medial Sound Substitution	27 (p. 28)	**Grade K** Lesson 9: Identify Medial Sounds in Spoken Words	18
	28 (p. 29)	**Grade 1** Lesson 2: Identify Medial Short Vowel Sounds in Spoken Single-Syllable Words	4
		Lesson 4: Identify Medial Long Vowel Sounds in Spoken Single-Syllable Words	8
		Grade 2 Lesson 2: Identify Medial Short Vowel Sounds in Spoken Single-Syllable Words	4
		Lesson 4: Identify Medial Long Vowel Sounds in Spoken Single-Syllable Words	8
Phoneme Addition	29 (p. 30)	**Grade K** Lesson 13: Produce a Spoken Word When Sounds Are Added or Substituted	26
	30 (p. 31)	**Grade 1** Lesson 19: Produce a Spoken Word When Sounds Are Added or Substituted	38
		Grade 2 Lesson 19: Produce a Spoken Word When Sounds Are Added or Substituted	38

Name _____ Date _____

Directions: Say the pair of words and ask the student if the words rhyme. If the student answers correctly, place a check mark (✓) in the scoring column. If the student's response is incorrect, make no mark. To find the total score, add the number of check marks.

Example: I will say the two words "book/look."
Then you will say if the words rhyme. (*yes*)

Word Pairs		Test Date _____	Test Date _____
1.	bug/rug (*yes*)		
2.	hop/hope (*no*)		
3.	jump/pump (*yes*)		
4.	tank/bank (*yes*)		
5.	floor/flow (*no*)		
6.	cub/cube (*no*)		
7.	wait/late (*yes*)		
8.	toss/floss (*yes*)		
9.	fog/fall (*no*)		
10.	catch/couch (*no*)		
Score		/10	/10

Comments/Observations: _____

_____

_____

Name _____ Date _____

Directions: Say the words in the set and have the student say the two words that rhyme. If the student answers correctly, place a check mark (✓) in the scoring column. If the student's response is incorrect, circle the words the student chose. To find the total score, add the number of check marks.

Example: I will say the three words "cup/duck/tuck."
Then you will pick which two words rhyme. (*duck, tuck*)

Word Sets	Test Date _____	Test Date _____
1. cake/take/neck (*cake, take*)		
2. kid/mad/lid (*kid, lid*)		
3. tap/let/nap (*tap, nap*)		
4. duck/rock/sock (*rock, sock*)		
5. nod/net/bet (*net, bet*)		
6. fun/sun/den (*fun, sun*)		
7. bell/call/sell (*bell, sell*)		
8. hood/good/head (*hood, good*)		
9. back/lick/sick (*lick, sick*)		
10. let/lot/spot (*lot, spot*)		
Score	/10	/10

Comments/Observations: _____

_____

_____

Name _____ Date _____

Directions: Read each sentence. Ask the student to give a real or nonsense word that rhymes with the last word in the sentence. If the student answers correctly, place a check mark (✓) in the scoring column. If the student's response is incorrect, write the word the student says. To find the total score, add the number of check marks.

Example: She has red hair.
      Tell me a word that rhymes with "hair." (*bear, fair . . .*)

Sentences	Test Date _____	Test Date _____
1. This is a nice day. Tell me a word that rhymes with "day." (*say, may . . .*)		
2. Mr. Smith has a pen. Tell me a word that rhymes with "pen." (*hen, men . . .*)		
3. Mom went to the store. Tell me a word that rhymes with "store." (*for, door . . .*)		
4. The dog chased the ball. Tell me a word that rhymes with "ball." (*tall, wall . . .*)		
5. That flower is pink. Tell me a word that rhymes with "pink." (*sink, think . . .*)		
6. Turn on the hose. Tell me a word that rhymes with "hose." (*rose, nose . . .*)		
Score	**/6**	**/6**

Comments/Observations: _____

_____

_____

Name _____ Date _____

Directions: Say the rhyming pair. Then ask the student to say another real or nonsense word that rhymes with the pair. If the student answers correctly, place a check mark (✓) in the scoring column. If the student's response is incorrect, write the word the student says. To find the total score, add the number of check marks.

Example: I will say the rhyming words "climb/lime."
Then you will give me a word that rhymes with the pair. (*time*)

Word Pairs	Test Date _____	Test Date _____
1. lash/mash (*rash, dash* . . .)		
2. not/dot (*lot, pot* . . .)		
3. lake/make (*take, bake* . . .)		
4. belt/pelt (*melt, felt* . . .)		
5. must/trust (*dust, crust* . . .)		
6. small/fall (*wall, ball* . . .)		
7. skunk/trunk (*hunk, junk* . . .)		
8. show/crow (*low, mow* . . .)		
9. thrill/chill (*fill, bill* . . .)		
Score	/9	/9

Comments/Observations: _____

_____

_____

Name _____ Date _____

Directions: Read each sentence. Ask the student to say the two words in the sentence that rhyme. If the student answers correctly, place a check mark (✓) in the scoring column. If the student's response is incorrect, circle the words the student says. To find the total score, add the number of check marks.

Example: We will get more at the store. (*more, store*)

Sentences		Test Date _____	Test Date _____
1.	The big brown dog jumped over the log. (*dog/log*)		
2.	Please help me plant the trees. (*please, trees*)		
3.	At the zoo, a cow said moo. (*zoo/moo*)		
4.	After I sweep, I am going to sleep. (*sweep, sleep*)		
5.	Were you able to clear the table? (*able, table*)		
6.	It costs a dime to buy a lime. (*dime, lime*)		
	Score	/6	/6

Comments/Observations: _____

_____

_____

Name _____ Date _____

Directions: Read each sentence. Ask the student to give a rhyming word for the specified word in the sentence. If the student answers correctly, place a check mark (✓) in the scoring column. If the student's response is incorrect, write the word the student says. To find the total score, add the number of check marks.

Example: "Put on your hat." Tell me a word that rhymes with "hat."
(*bat, cat...*)

Sentences	Test Date _____	Test Date _____
1. "That frog can jump." Tell me a word that rhymes with "frog." (*log, dog . . .*)		
2. "We went to the lake." Tell me a word that rhymes with "lake." (*make, rake . . .*)		
3. "There is a crack in the wall." Tell me a word that rhymes with "crack." (*back, tack . . .*)		
4. "The cat likes to play." Tell me a word that rhymes with "play." (*day, ray . . .*)		
5. "The little girl waved." Tell me a word that rhymes with "girl." (*curl, twirl . . .*)		
6. "She can win the race." Tell me a word that rhymes with "race." (*face, lace . . .*)		
Score	/6	/6

Comments/Observations: _____

_____

_____

Name _____ Date _____

Directions: Say the word. Have the student repeat the word and tell you the beginning sound. If the student answers correctly, place a check mark (✓) in the scoring column. If the student's response is incorrect, record the error. To find the total score, add the number of check marks.

Example: I will say the word "book."
Repeat the word and tell me the beginning sound.
book (/b/)

Words		Test Date _____	Test Date _____
1.	sink (/s/)		
2.	boat (/b/)		
3.	month (/m/)		
4.	hoop (/h/)		
5.	leg (/l/)		
6.	turtle (/t/)		
7.	goose (/g/)		
8.	pudding (/p/)		
Score		/8	/8

Comments/Observations: _____

_____

_____

Grades K–2 • Benchmark Advance • **Phonological Awareness** Quick Checks • © Benchmark Education Company, LLC

Name _____ Date _____

Directions: Say the word. Have the student repeat the word and tell you the middle sound. If the student answers correctly, place a check mark (✓) in the scoring column. If the student's response is incorrect, record the error. To find the total score, add the number of check marks.

Example: I will say the word "hat."
Repeat the word "hat" and tell me its middle sound.
(*Hat. I hear /a/ in the middle of the word "hat."*)

Words	Test Date _____	Test Date _____
1. pet (*/e/*)		
2. sack (*/a/*)		
3. hit (*/i/*)		
4. stop (*/o/*)		
5. cut (*/u/*)		

Directions: Say the word. Have the student repeat the word and tell you the ending sound.

Example: I will say the word "bit."
Repeat the word "bit" and tell me its ending sound.
(*Bit. I hear /t/ at the end of the word "bit."*)

6. lake (*/k/*)		
7. road (*/d/*)		
8. size (*/z/*)		
9. cup (*/p/*)		
10. man (*/n/*)		
Score	/10	/10

Comments/Observations: _____

_____

_____

Name _____ Date _____

Directions: Say the first sound of the word, followed by the rest of the word. Then have the student say the whole word. If the student answers correctly, place a check mark (✓) in the scoring column. If the student's response is incorrect, record the error. To find the total score, add the number of check marks.

Example: I will say the first sound of a word, followed by the rest. Say the word that I just sounded out. (/l/ /ip/ *lip*)

Words	Test Date _____	Test Date _____
1. /p/ /in/ (*pin*)		
2. /r/ /ub/ (*rub*)		
3. /s/ /it/ (*sit*)		
4. /m/ /an/ (*man*)		
5. /n/ /ap/ (*nap*)		
6. /f/ /un/ (*fun*)		
7. /h/ /ot/ (*hot*)		
8. /s/ /ad/ (*sad*)		
9. /d/ /eck/ (*deck*)		
10. /b/ /ill/ (*bill*)		
Score	/10	/10

Comments/Observations: _____

_____

_____

Name _____ Date _____

Directions: Say the first sound of the word, and then say the rest of the word. Have the student repeat the word. If the student answers correctly, place a check mark (✓) in the scoring column. If the student's response is incorrect, record the error. To find the total score, add the number of check marks.

Example: I will say the first sound of a word, followed by the rest. Say the word that I just sounded out. (/k/ /ap/ *cap*)

Words	Test Date _____	Test Date _____
1. /b/ /id/ (*bid*)		
2. /l/ /ot (*lot*)		
3. /m/ /iss/ (*miss*)		
4. /w/ /ash/ (*wash*)		
5. /f/ /el/ (*fell*)		
6. /t/ /ak/ (*tack*)		
7. /r/ /ug/ (*rug*)		
8. /k/ ost/ (*cost*)		
9. /l/ /ēp/ (*leap*)		
10. /s/ /ing/ (*sing*)		
Score	/10	/10

Comments/Observations: _____

_____

_____

Name _____ Date _____

Directions: Say the first syllable of the word, followed by the rest of the word. Have the student say the whole word. If the student answers correctly, place a check mark (✓) in the scoring column. If the student's response is incorrect, record the error. To find the total score, add the number of check marks.

Example: I will say the first syllable of a word, followed by the rest: do-nut. Say the word that I just sounded out. (*donut*)

Words	Test Date _____	Test Date _____
1. fun-ny (*funny*)		
2. o-pen (*open*)		
3. doc-tor (*doctor*)		
4. be-gin (*begin*)		
5. help-er (*helper*)		
6. un-til (*until*)		
7. jack-et (*jacket*)		
8. lit-tle (*little*)		
Score	/8	/8

Comments/Observations: _____

_____

_____

Name _____ Date _____

Directions: Say the first syllable of the word, followed by the rest of the word. Have the student say the whole word. If the student answers correctly, place a check mark (✓) in the scoring column. If the student's response is incorrect, record the error. To find the total score, add the number of check marks.

Example: I will say the first syllable of a word, followed by the rest: ear-ly. Say the word that I just sounded out. (*early*)

Words		Test Date _____	Test Date _____
1.	lock-er (*locker*)		
2.	ta-ble (*table*)		
3.	kit-ten (*kitten*)		
4.	mu-sic (*music*)		
5.	win-ter (*winter*)		
6.	la-dy (*lady*)		
7.	bor-row (*borrow*)		
8.	cal-en-dar (*calendar*)		
Score		/8	/8

Comments/Observations: _____

_____

_____

Name _____ Date _____

Directions: Say the word. Have the student tell you all of the sounds in the word. If the student answers correctly, place a check mark (✓) in the scoring column. If the student's response is incorrect, record the error. To find the total score, add the number of check marks.

Example: If I say "fun," you say /f/ /u/ /n/.

Words		Test Date _____	Test Date _____
1.	hot (/h/ /o/ /t/)		
2.	win (/w/ /i/ /n/)		
3.	rub (/r/ /u/ /b/)		
4.	tap (/t/ /a/ /p/)		
5.	men (/m/ /e/ /n/)		
6.	said (/s/ /e/ /d/)		
7.	cup (/k/ /u/ /p/)		
8.	bag (/b/ /a/ /g/)		
Score		/8	/8

Comments/Observations: _____

_____

_____

Name _____ Date _____

Directions: Say the word. Have the student tell you all of the sounds in the word. If the student answers correctly, place a check mark (✓) in the scoring column. If the student's response is incorrect, record the error. To find the total score, add the number of check marks.

Example: If I say "back," you say /b/ /a/ /k/.

Words		Test Date _____	Test Date _____
1.	him (/h/ /i/ /m/)		
2.	rope (/r/ /ō/ /p/)		
3.	goose (/g/ /oo̅/ /s/)		
4.	queen (/kw/ /ē/ /n/)		
5.	thin (/th/ /i/ /n/)		
6.	shop (/sh/ /o/ /p/)		
7.	raise (/r/ /ā/ /z/)		
8.	buzz (/b/ /u/ /z/)		
9.	sock (/s/ /o/ /k/)		
10.	right (/r/ /ī/ /t/)		
Score		/10	/10

Comments/Observations: _____

_____

_____

Name _____ Date _____

Directions: Say the set of words and tell the student a sound. Have the student say the two words that have the sound. If the student answers correctly, place a check mark (✓) in the scoring column. If the student's response is incorrect, record the error. To find the total score, add the number of check marks.

Example: I will say the words "rich," "rice," "bite."
Tell me which words have the /ī/ sound. (*rice, bite*)

Word Sets	Test Date _____	Test Date _____
1. boat, him, home Which words have the /ō/ sound? (*boat, home*)		
2. mouse, tie, late Which words have the /t/ sound? (*tie, late*)		
3. bottle, bake, tape Which words have the /ā/ sound? (*bake, tape*)		
4. zoo, froze, sock Which words have the /z/ sound? (*zoo, froze*)		
5. chin, reach, sick Which words have the /ch/ sound? (*chin, reach*)		
6. us, mop, cup Which words have the /u/ sound? (*us, cup*)		
Score	/6	/6

Comments/Observations: _____

_____

_____

Name _____ Date _____

Directions: Say the pair of words and ask the student which sound is in both words. If the student answers correctly, place a check mark (✓) in the scoring column. If the student's response is incorrect, record the error. To find the total score, add the number of check marks.

Example: I will say the words "ride" and "bike."
Which sound is in both words? (/ī/)

Word Pairs	Test Date _____	Test Date _____
1. hole, boat Which sound is in both words? (/ō/)		
2. tin, sign Which sound is in both words? (/n/)		
3. sap, miss Which sound is in both words? (/s/)		
4. pot, pair Which sound is in both words? (/p/)		
5. kite, deck Which sound is in both words? (/k/)		
6. home, have Which sound is in both words? (/h/)		
7. beat, reed Which sound is in both words? (/ē/)		
Score	**/7**	**/7**

Comments/Observations: _____

_____

_____

Name _____ Date _____

Directions: Say the word. Ask the student to replace the beginning sound with the new sound to make a different word. If the student answers correctly, place a check mark (✓) in the scoring column. If the student's response is incorrect, record the error. To find the total score, add the number of check marks.

Example: The word is "kit." I will change /k/ to /p/.
Say the new word. (*pit*)

Words	Test Date _____	Test Date _____
1. tick: change /t/ to /l/ What is the new word? (*lick*)		
2. ride: change /r/ to /t/ What is the new word? (*tide*)		
3. fun: change /f/ to /b/ What is the new word? (*bun*)		
4. sail: change /s/ to /m/ What is the new word? (*mail*)		
5. rope: change /r/ to /h/ What is the new word? (*hope*)		
6. poor: change /p/ to /d/ What is the new word? (*door*)		
Score	/6	/6

Comments/Observations: _____

_____

_____

Name _____ Date _____

Directions: Say the word. Ask the student to replace the beginning sound with the new sound to make a different word. If the student answers correctly, place a check mark (✓) in the scoring column. If the student's response is incorrect, record the error. To find the total score, add the number of check marks.

Example: The word is "sell." I will change /s/ to /w/.
Say the new word. (*well*)

Words	Test Date _____	Test Date _____
1. boil: change /b/ to /f/ What is the new word? (*foil*)		
2. sip: change /s/ to /wh/ What is the new word? (*whip*)		
3. low: change /l/ to /kr/ What is the new word? (*crow*)		
4. pink: change /p/ to /th/ What is the new word? (*think*)		
5. rake: change /r/ to /sn/ What is the new word? (*snake*)		
6. pat: change /p/ to /ch/ What is the new word? (*chat*)		
Score	/6	/6

Comments/Observations: _____

_____

_____

Name _____ Date _____

Directions: Say the words. Ask the student to tell you the two words that begin with the same sound. If the student answers correctly, place a check mark (✓) in the scoring column. If the student's response is incorrect, record the error. To find the total score, add the number of check marks.

Example: I will say the words "lump/loose/shore."
Tell me which two words begin with the same sound.
(*lump, loose*)

Word Sets	Test Date _____	Test Date _____
1. new/number/tall (*new, number*)		
2. face/tunnel/fun (*face, fun*)		
3. teach/soup/south (*soup, south*)		
4. many/moon/soft (*many, moon*)		
5. gate/mother/guess (*gate, guess*)		
6. piano/cake/push (*piano, push*)		
7. today/note/tool (*today, tool*)		
8. cart/money/come (*cart, come*)		
9. size/zoo/super (*size, super*)		
10. egg/up/enter (*egg, enter*)		
Score	/10	/10

Comments/Observations: _____

_____

_____

Name _____ Date _____

Directions: Read the sentence. Ask the student to tell you the two words that begin with the same sound. If the student answers correctly, place a check mark (✓) in the scoring column. If the student's response is incorrect, record the error. To find the total score, add the number of check marks.

Example: Listen to the sentence: The goose got away.
Tell me which two words begin with the same sound.
(*goose*, *got*)

Sentences	Test Date _____	Test Date _____
1. We played in the sand by the sea. (*sand*, *sea*)		
2. A cat came into the room. (*cat*, *came*)		
3. The book had a bad ending. (*book*, *bad*)		
4. She made this with milk. (*made*, *milk*)		
5. Dad will shop for a new shirt. (*shop*, *shirt*)		
Score	/5	/5

Comments/Observations: _____

_____

_____

Name _____ Date _____

Directions: Say the word. Have the student repeat the word and clap for the number of syllables. If the student answers correctly, place a check mark (✓) in the scoring column. If the student's response is incorrect, record the error. To find the total score, add the number of check marks.

Example: I will say the word "engine." Repeat the word and clap out the number of syllables (*en-gine, <two>*)

Words	Test Date _____	Test Date _____
1. told (*told, <one>*)		
2. reading (*read-ing, <two>*)		
3. movement (*move-ment, <two>*)		
4. dishwasher (*dish-wash-er, <three>*)		
5. science (*sci-ence, <two>*)		
6. television (*tel-e-vi-sion, <four>*)		
7. celebrate (*cel-e-brate, <three>*)		
Score	/7	/7

Comments/Observations: _____

_____

_____

Name _____ Date _____

Directions: Say the word. Have the student repeat the word and tell you the number of syllables in the word. If the student answers correctly, place a check mark (✓) in the scoring column. If the student's response is incorrect, record the error. To find the total score, add the number of check marks.

Example: I will say the word "apron." Repeat the word and tell me the number of syllables in the word. (*a-pron*, *two syllables*)

Words	Test Date _____	Test Date _____
1. maple (*ma-ple*, *two*)		
2. yesterday (*yes-ter-day*, *three*)		
3. closing (*clos-ing*, *two*)		
4. strength (*strength*, *one*)		
5. waterfall (*wa-ter-fall*, *three*)		
6. hurry (*hur-ry*, *two*)		
7. beautiful (*beau-ti-ful*, *three*)		
Score	/7	/7

Comments/Observations: _____

_____

_____

Name _____ Date _____

Directions: Say the sounds of a word. Have the student blend the sounds and say the word. If the child answers correctly, place a check mark (✓) in the scoring column. If the student's response is incorrect, record the error. To find the total score, add the number of check marks.

Example: I will say the sounds /b/ /i/ /t/.
Now, blend the sounds together and say the word. (*bit*)

Word Sounds	Test Date _____	Test Date _____
1. /d/ /o/ /t/ (*dot*)		
2. /s/ /a/ /p/ (*sap*)		
3. /k/ /o/ /b/ (*cob*)		
4. /d/ /e/ /n/ (*den*)		
5. /r/ /e/ /d/ (*red*)		
6. /m/ /i/ /x/ (*mix*)		
7. /b/ /u/ /s/ (*bus*)		
8. /w/ /e/ /t/ (*wet*)		
9. /j/ /u/ /g/ (*jug*)		
10. /h/ /a/ /t/ (*hat*)		
Score	/10	/10

Comments/Observations: _____

_____

_____

Name _____ Date _____

Directions: Say the sounds of a word. Have the student blend the sounds and say the word. If the student answers correctly, place a check mark (✓) in the scoring column. If the student's response is incorrect, record the error. To find the total score, add the number of check marks.

Example: I will say the sounds /s/ /i/ /p/.
　　　　　　Now, blend the sounds together and say the word. (*sip*)

Word Sounds	Test Date _____	Test Date _____
1.　　/g/ /u/ /m/ (*gum*)		
2.　　/k/ /o͝o/ /d/ (*could*)		
3.　　/sl/ /e/ /d/ (*sled*)		
4.　　/r/ /i/ /ng/ (*ring*)		
5.　　/h/ /a/ /p/ /ē/ (*happy*)		
6.　　/w/ /ô/ /k/ (*walk*)		
7.　　/m/ /o͞o/ /n/ (*moon*)		
8.　　/b/ /ē/ /t/ (*beet*)		
9.　　/r/ /a/ /p/ (*rap*)		
10.　/j/ /ō/ /k/ (*joke*)		
Score	**/10**	**/10**

Comments/Observations: _____

_____

_____

Name _____ Date _____

Directions: Say the word. Ask the student to replace the ending sound with the new sound to make a different word. If the student answers correctly, place a check mark (✓) in the scoring column. If the student's response is incorrect, record the error. To find the total score, add the number of check marks.

Example: I will say the word "kit." You will replace the ending sound /t/ with the new sound /d/ to make a different word. (*kid*)

Words	Test Date _____	Test Date _____
1. lip: change /p/ to /k/ What is the new word? (*lick*)		
2. cub: change /b/ to /f/ What is the new word? (*cuff*)		
3. game: change /m/ to /t/ What is the new word? (*gate*)		
4. road: change /d/ to /m/ What is the new word? (*roam*)		
5. peach: change /ch/ to /k/ What is the new word? (*peak*)		
6. chin: change /n/ to /p/ What is the new word? (*chip*)		
Score	**/6**	**/6**

Comments/Observations: _____

_____

_____

Name _____ Date _____

Directions: Say the word. Ask the student to replace the ending sound with the new sound to make a different word. If the student answers correctly, place a check mark (✓) in the scoring column. If the student's response is incorrect, record the error. To find the total score, add the number of check marks.

Example: I will say the word "spin." You will replace the ending sound /n/ with the new sound /t/ to make a different word. (*spit*)

Words	Test Date _____	Test Date _____
1. pet: change /t/ to /n/ (*pen*)		
2. trip: change /p/ to /m/ (*trim*)		
3. mad: change /d/ to /sh/ (*mash*)		
4. floss: change /s/ to /p/ (*flop*)		
5. blog: change /g/ to /t/ (*blot*)		
6. sub: change /b/ to /ch/ (*such*)		
Score	/6	/6

Comments/Observations: _____

_____

_____

Name _____ Date _____

Directions: Say the word. Ask the student to replace the middle sound with the new sound to make a different word. If the student answers correctly, place a check mark (✓) in the scoring column. If the student's response is incorrect, record the error. To find the total score, add the number of check marks.

Example: I will say the word "mop." You will replace the middle sound /o/ with the new sound /a/ to make a different word. (*map*)

Words	Test Date _____	Test Date _____
1. fix: change /i/ to /o/ (*fox*)		
2. rag: change /a/ to /u/ (*rug*)		
3. sock: change /o/ to /i/ (*sick*)		
4. vet: change /e/ to /ō/ (*vote*)		
5. lake: change /ā/ to /ī/ (*like*)		
6. miss: change /i/ to /ī/ (*mice*)		
Score	/6	/6

Comments/Observations: _____

_____

_____

Name _____ Date _____

Directions: Say the word. Ask the student to replace the middle sound with the new sound to make a different word. If the student answers correctly, place a check mark (✓) in the scoring column. If the student's response is incorrect, record the error. To find the total score, add the number of check marks.

Example: I will say the word "let." You will replace the middle sound /e/ with the new sound /i/ to make a different word. (*lit*)

Words	Test Date _____	Test Date _____
1. tub: change /u/ to /a/ (*tab*)		
2. can: change /a/ to /o/ (*cone*)		
3. foil: change /oi/ to /aw/ (*fall*)		
4. bay: change /ā/ to /oi/ (*boy*)		
5. dome: change /ō/ to /ī/ (*dime*)		
6. slap: change /a/ to /ē/ (*sleep*)		
Score	/6	/6

Comments/Observations: _____

_____

_____

Name _____ Date _____

Directions: Say the word, and then segment it sound by sound.
Ask the student to add a sound to the beginning of the word and say the
new word. If the student answers correctly, place a check mark (✓) in the
scoring column. If the student's response is incorrect, record the error.
To find the total score, add the number of check marks.

Example: I will say the word "in" and say its sounds /i/ /n/. You will add
the /b/ sound to the beginning of the word and then say the
new word. (*bin*)

Words	Test Date _____	Test Date _____
1. arm /a/ /r/ /m/ Add /f/ to the beginning of the word. (*farm*)		
2. earn /er/ /n/ Add /l/ to the beginning of the word. (*learn*)		
3. lip /l/ /i/ /p/ Add /s/ to the beginning of the word. (*slip*)		
4. ore /or/ Add /m/ to the beginning of the word. (*more*)		
5. ring /r/ /i/ /ng/ Add /b/ to the beginning of the word. (*bring*)		
Score	/5	/5

Comments/Observations: _____

_____

_____

Name _____ Date _____

Directions: Say the word, and then segment it sound by sound. Ask the student to add a sound to the end of the word and say the new word. If the student answers correctly, place a check mark (✓) in the scoring column. If the student's response is incorrect, record the error. To find the total score, add the number of check marks.

Example: I will say the word "pin" and say its sounds /p/ /i/ /n/. You will add the sound /k/ to the end of the word and then say the new word. (*pink*)

Words	Test Date _____	Test Date _____
1. car /k/ /ar/ Add /t/ to the end of the word. (*cart*)		
2. for /f/ /or/ Add /k/ to the end of the word. (*fork*)		
3. tea /t/ /ē/ Add /m/ to the end of the word. (*team*)		
4. dam /d/ /a/ /m/ Add /p/ to the end of the word. (*damp*)		
5. men /m/ /e/ /n/ Add /d/ to the end of the word. (*mend*)		
Score	/5	/5

Comments/Observations: _____

_____

_____